The Lunar Key

The Lunar Key

An Adventure in Understanding Your Dreams

Kym Maehl, PhD

Carson City, Nevada, USA

Cover Art: Jake Branco

Author Photo: Laurie Bray Photography

ISBN-13: 978-0692327432
ISBN-10:   0692327436

Printed in the United States of America.

Contents

Acknowledgements

I have so much gratitude for all those along the way who have helped awaken the dreamer in me. I thank my husband, Ron, who has taken this journey with me many times before and who in this lifetime has challenged and encouraged me to open to the highest expression of my life's purpose. I also thank my sister, Keri, who stands beside me as healer, sister and friend, and who too has been my companion in many lifetimes. I thank Nancy Epstein for transcribing hour upon hour of dream interpretations that were used as the foundation for this book. And I especially thank Deana Hoover for her dreams, her editing, and her willingness to open herself for all to see. Without all of the love and support that I have received from each of you, this book would be an untapped gem bouncing around in my head. Thank you! You have helped me realize my dream.

9

Forward – The Lunar Key

I chose the title and the cover art for this book following a generous gift given to me by artist, Jake Branco. Jake gifted me his painting in exchange for a past life regression, which I facilitated for him. At the time, Jake knew nothing about this project or my love for dream interpretation. He only knew that he was grateful for the work that we'd done together and that he wanted to show his gratitude.

The moment I saw the painting, I knew that it would be the cover for my book and I immediately called it, *The Lunar Key*. Jake was surprised because he had called it *Lunar Tear*. This was equally surprising to me, because I hadn't even noticed the tear; I had only seen the key.

In Divine synchronicity, either name would have been perfect for a book about dreaming. Like the moon, dreams take us into a deeper, more intuitive part of ourselves and illuminate messages being sent from our subconscious mind. Like this book, the key is an instrument that helps to unlock what is encrypted in the message. And like the tear, emotional release occurs, both happy and sad when we experience the feeling of the message. Each of these is perfect for the intention of this book.

I stayed with *The Lunar Key* because I see the key as a symbol that signifies the potential of unlocking the mysterious language of our dreams. And, as you will see in the pages that follow, there is both personal and transpersonal significance to symbols, such as the key, that can bring us into a deeper understanding of Self.

Flowing with the theme of unlocking the inner depths for deeper understanding, it is my intention to take a topic that has been obscured and enigmatic and make it approachable, applicable and fun. I hope you will be touched by the vulnerability of the dreams that are shared and the richness of what is experienced, both heartbreaking and joyous. I hope you will laugh with me and cry with me, knowing that in that space of our humanness, we are one. We are connected by a transcendent thread that has brought us together in this brief span of time to remind us that we are more than just body and mind, we are spirit as well. As spiritual beings, we are all connected and our dreams are there to help us follow the stream of that connection.

In following the stream into the depths of our dreams, we discover, we feel, we unlock the secrets and the mysteries of not only our subconscious minds, but of all consciousness. This allows us to traverse the personal and transpersonal alike. Our dreams, therefore, become the vehicles that take us out of the dark of unknowing and into the light of awareness.

As we connect on this journey together it is my deepest desire that you might find a key that opens what may have been locked on your adventure into self-discovery. It is also my hope that together we may share the satisfaction of breaking the code, and interpreting the language, of your subconscious mind as out-pictured in your dreams.

Introduction – A Dream

I was walking through the rooms of a small house that my sister and her family were living in while she and my parents were building her new home. I walked to the sliding glass door in the back of the house where her oldest son, Will, and a friend were standing. I didn't know the other boy, but both he and Will were about 16. Will was funny and was asking my sister if he could have the car. She told him no, that he would have to earn gas money first. This didn't seem to bother Will and he just shrugged his shoulders and walked away with his friend. I stared at him and felt so frustrated because while he was there I wanted to talk to him but couldn't think of anything to say.

.....I woke with tears in my eyes and still feel the sting of those tears as I write. You see, this was a dream and Will, my 24 year old nephew, had just died two months earlier…

I start with this because dreams like this are the reason that I do dream work. They are rich with information that lingers in the conscious and subconscious mind that still needs to be acknowledged or processed. For me, this dream was a combination of the memory of my nephew when he was still so fresh and filled with potential. But even more was the deeply seated feeling of frustration that I have now that I want to tell him something, but feel like I can't because he's no longer in his body.

My existential knowing of the Soul's journey is so much greater than this, but the human part of me sometimes gets caught in the limitation of linear existence. Thanks to dreams like this, I am reminded of the denseness of the emotional body and I am continuing to process what arises.

From this, you might guess that this project is going to be part of my healing journey, one that I would like to invite you on. It will be both personal and transpersonal, because those things with the highest truth are as true for one as they are for many. And nestled deeply within our subconscious minds and delivered to us in our dreams is the wisdom to expand, to heal, and to grow if we just take the time to listen.

I dedicate this book to Will and to Sadie, who you will hear about later, for breaking our hearts open so wide that we could reach within the depths of our beings for healing and truth. In doing so, we begin to remove the veil of separation and enter into the suspended space where all souls and memories remain connected. In that space, the magical space of our dreams, we are unfettered by what we perceive as reality. We are the Spirit of imagination. Linear time ceases to exist and we are free to rediscover that which was never truly lost.

Chapter One – The Basics of Dream Work

Dreams, the great multi-dimensional experience, the great multi-dimensional adventure... I first got interested in dreaming and wanting to understand my dreams when I was in my teens. I used to have what I now know were recurring theme dreams in which I was scared. The scenes varied but the essence was the same. I would be trying to jump off the ground and fly, to get away, and something was always chasing me, pulling at me, trying to keep me down. At that time, I didn't really understand what these dreams were about but I knew that when I had them, I would carry the feeling of fear around with me for days after the dream. Eventually, this lead me to the study of dreams and dream interpretation.

Like many, I began with dream interpretation books and started working with their definitions of symbols. While they made some sense, they didn't always feel quite right.

It wasn't until later in my life when I entered into more transpersonal work, namely breathwork, that I started to get a greater sense or knowing that dreams have a language all their own and that the language, definitions, and symbolism that I was reading in the dream books wasn't necessarily mine. This prompted me to work more closely with my own dreams and to uncover my own dream language.

Since then, almost 30 years later, I have used what I've discovered to help clients understand the value and meaning of their dreams and how they can apply that information in their lives. This book, *"The Lunar Key - An Adventure in Understanding Your Dreams,"* was born out of that work.

What I have found from my experience, my studies and my work with clients is that when we can understand the language of our dreams, we begin to understand a deeper part of our being. This project approaches dreams in that way. It is not specifically about just finding out the simple or the mundane explanation of our dreams, although that can be part of it. Moreover, it's about understanding the depth of the information that our subconscious mind is giving us so that we can heal, grow, and become more actualized as both human and spiritual beings.

For this reason, it is important to understand that we all dream. Each and every one of us dreams, and while there are those who claim they don't, research has determined that we all have between three and six dreams a night. Those that say they do not dream simply don't remember them. This is a significant point because whether we remember them or not, our dreams play an important role in our mental, emotional and spiritual wellbeing.

Dreams are a valuable part of our psychospiricology, a wonderful word, if it were an actual word rather than one that I decided to make up to prepare you for the upcoming Deana dreams. If it were an actual word, it would refer to the personal and transpersonal nature of dreaming and thus its immense value to our essential self and our sense of who we are. Getting to know our essential self is paramount to self-actualization, as well as a deeper connection with something higher than ourselves.

Purpose & Value of Dreaming -

From this holistic, mind-body-spirit perspective, dreams have several purposes. First, they help us to explore alternate realms that we may not be open to or even be aware of in our conscious waking reality. When dreaming, our subconscious mind is open to all that is and is free to travel to those places, those dimensions or realities. Whether imagined or real, these various dimensions are rich with symbolic information that can help us in the further exploration of self.

In addition to other realms, dreams also help us to access all memories housed within our subconscious minds. These memories contain current, recent past, multigenerational, and even past life information that influences who we are and how we navigate our lives. When this information inserts itself into our dreamtime, it provides a glimpse into these motivating factors and gives us the opportunity to make what is unconscious,

conscious.

Dreams also help us to release energy that may have been pent up throughout the day and that was not adequately processed while awake. There's a great value to this because it helps that energy to be released before it becomes locked down in the body to manifest in one's biology as distress or dis-ease.

Similar to this, dreams also provide a vehicle for processing feelings and emotions that we didn't or couldn't process in our conscious waking reality. This is akin to the fear dreams that I talked about earlier and that stimulated my interest in understanding the meaning of dreams. Remember when I kept dreaming of being chased by something or someone that was grabbing at me and keeping me from flying? Well, as I began working with the meaning of these dreams and the feelings they evoked, I came to realize that I was holding a deep subconscious fear of not being able to get off the ground and do what I've come into this life to do. Only with that awareness was I able to intentionally work through that fear and re-script the underlying beliefs. The dreams didn't clear the fear or the beliefs. However, they were instrumental in helping me become aware of emotions that may not have reached full awareness in my conscious mind but that were actively working beneath the surface in my subconscious mind. With that awareness and subsequent clearing work, rarely, if ever, has that particular set of theme dreams resurfaced.

In addition to helping experience other realities and memories, and to clear energy or emotions, dreams also provide us with clues into deeper parts of ourselves and what we may need for higher functioning. Through the use of symbols and themes, our subconscious mind conveys messages through our dreams that can help us understand ourselves better. As just discussed, one of my early life themes was the fear of failure, particularly as it applied to the inability to do my life's work. While in the example above, I experienced this theme through a recurring dream sequence, important ideas can also be conveyed through symbols, such as houses, trees or fires, all of which we'll be talking about later. For now, it is important to recognize that symbols are the way that the subconscious mind speaks to us. They are profoundly significant, and yet often frequently overlooked in the overall story of the dream.

What makes symbols significant is the meaning that we assign to them. These meanings can be personal, universal or archetypal and are rich with information. A personal symbol might mean something to one person and something else to another. A universal symbol, on the other hand, has an assigned meaning that is the same for most people within a similar framework. An archetypal symbol is one that is present in the collective psyche and is therefore the same for all people. Recognizing these symbols as they present themselves and giving them meaning helps us to create continuity in the flow of the dream and ultimately in understanding the language of the subconscious mind.

It is valuable therefore to become aware of our own dream language and to listen to what our subconscious is telling us. One important message for me was to lighten up and relax. Whenever I had a dream that seemed unimportant, simply fun and frivolous, I learned that I was being told that my nervous system needed a chance to unwind and to take the opportunity to open to my imagination and play.

For much of my early life, I had placed so many restrictions on myself that my dreams became a way for me to step out of the box for awhile and learn more about parts of myself that I wasn't allowing to express. With that awareness, I have been able to intentionally integrate more creative expression into my life and play more. This in turn has lead to greater mental, physical and spiritual health, and a whole lot more laughter.

In whatever way they present themselves, our dreams are most useful to us when we give them our attention and place significance on their messages. As we do this, we are rewarded with more information, more dreams and more awareness about ourselves and the multi-dimensionality of life.

Types of Dreams –

As we begin to recognize the purpose and the value of our dreams, it is useful to understand the types of dreams that we have. In my work, I generally see four main types of dreams. The first is what I call the *simple* or the *direct dream*. These are narratives that can be taken at face value, meaning that if you are having a dream about wanting to eat cake because you're on a diet, you might just want to eat cake. These dreams are great because they help us to simply step into our dreams. They're not too difficult to understand and they make sense. They also help us to make a quick and easy association with the dream and what's happening when we're awake.

The next type of dream is what I call *imagery* or *inspiration dreams*. These are the narratives that just cut loose and let us have experiences that we would never have in our waking state. What's wonderful about these types of dreams is that they give us permission to explore other possibilities more, because, if we can dream it, we can become it. While it may not have the exact physical or literal manifestation that was presented in the dream, the feelings and insights are the same and thus the experience becomes qualitatively similar.

The third type of dream is what I call a *clearing dream*. These are dreams that help us to process information, energy or emotions that happened during waking hours but didn't get processed while awake. One example of this type of dream in my own life is what I call the "waitress nightmare." I worked as a waitress for a long time during and after college, and as such, experienced a lot of work-related stress that would reflect in my dreams. In these dreams, my tables would be packed, food was coming out wrong and I just couldn't get caught up...or something like that. And now, even though I haven't waited tables for nearly 30 years, I can still have a waitress nightmare every so often when there's a lot of chaos and stress going on in my daily life. When I have one of these dreams, I know that I am being told to pay attention to what's going on around me and to find a way to lighten the load and let go of stress.

The fourth type of dream is the *recurring dream*. These are dreams that we have over and over again and that are similar in some way each time we dream them. These are like the dreams that I referred to in the beginning where I had that sense of being chased and not being able to get off the ground. These were accompanied by the fear of not being able to get away. In this case, the details of the dreams weren't exactly the same but the theme and feeling was recurring. There was always a sense of wanting to jump up and fly and yet having something chasing me and pulling me down.

This recurring theme and subsequent dream would happen when there was something in my life that felt way off track or when I was feeling like I'd failed, which was a lot of the time. The issue was large enough for me that I kept having the dream over and over. This is because, when you have the same dream over and over again, it either says that you're continuing to have the same issue arise that hasn't yet been resolved fully, or that you're not dealing with the underlying energy of the issue so you require a powerful reminder.

What I know now that I didn't know then is that my feeling of failure was so strong that I kept manifesting more reasons to support the faulty belief. My dreams were telling me this through repetition. Therefore, the repetition of recurring dreams intensifies their significance because if the subconscious keeps sending the dream it is saying that this is a message that must be attended to for your personal wellbeing.

Finally, while I said that there are four main types of dreams that I usually encounter, there is another that is not as common, but is important to mention. These are what I call *prophetic dreams*, in which some or all of a dream will actually happen at a later time in conscious waking reality. Besides being able to observe the manifestation of the dream in reality, prophetic dreams can be discernable by the energy or feeling that accompanies them. Because there will be a unique quality or feeling to these dreams that is different than other dreams, it is useful to work closely enough with your dreams to become clear when this feeling or energy exists. By doing this, the information that is presented in the dream can be useful and/or observable. The challenge with these dreams is that even when you're aware of them, it can be confusing knowing what to do with the information. That is why when interpreting what appears to be a prophetic dream, as with other dreams, I generally direct the dreamer to view the dream as a reflection of self first and then consider its prophetic possibilities.

Getting to Know Your Dreams –

It is finding the "reflection of self" that leads us into dream interpretation. Having taken a look at the value and purpose of dreaming, as well as the different types of dreams, the stage is set for understanding what our dreams might mean. To do this, I ascribe to a Jungian perspective that looks at different parts of the dream as reflections of the dreamer, their consciousness, and/or what's going on in their current waking reality. Even when dreaming of another person, I will ask the dreamer how that person is a reflection of him or herself.

However, even before that, I will begin with tapping into

the dreamer's emotional body by asking how the dream made them feel. As a dreamer or facilitator, I start with the feeling because that is the densest part of the dream, and is therefore the part of the dream that usually stays with us the longest. Additionally, it helps to establish the tone of the dream, which may or may not be consistent with the imagery. For example, while dreaming of a monster, the feeling of the dream might be light and carefree versus scary and foreboding as you might expect. That would then lead the interpretation in a different direction.

Next, I start looking for the language that the dreamer uses because that always gives me cues about what's going on. It might lead to a direct reference, or it might lead to something metaphorical. It is then that I look and listen for objects that have symbolism that may be personal, universal or archetypal. Again, I will ask what the symbol or object means to the dreamer. And sometimes, if they are unsure, I will offer what it means to me and then ask them how that feels for them. Whatever approach, I always have them check in with their own feeling sense.

Because working with dreams is more intuitive than scientific, there is no "one way" that will lead you to the exact interpretation. Rather, it is more like looking for clues, with each part of the dream being another clue. For that reason, when I first start talking with a dreamer about possible interpretations, I might encourage them to get a dream interpretation book so that they can get a reference for what certain objects and symbols mean to someone else. This is not because those interpretations are "right," but because they give a suggestion or place to start.

I also find that it can be useful, for those really interested in working with their dreams, to keep a dream journal. Like a diary, a dream journal is a place to write down the important aspects of a dream, possibly including dates, times, thoughts, and feelings, both from and about the dream. These can be valuable in later reflection when looking for patterns and providing context for how they may be tied to ones waking experiences.

Furthermore, once a dreamer begins to keep track of their dreams, they will start to see the emergence of certain symbols that will repeat themselves and that will have a unique meaning to them. For this reason, I also encourage dreamers to compile a personal dream dictionary that makes reference to the meaning that they assign to the common symbols within their dreams.

In a dream journal or dream dictionary, it is not necessary to write lengthy narratives. In fact, I find that brief notes reflecting key points and standout items are most useful. This is true for two reasons. The first is that it is human nature to be more apt to keep track of dreams on a routine basis if it can be done quickly. If the practice takes too long and infringes upon other daily activities, the dreamer may forgo the time it takes and do other things.

The second reason brief is better is that frequently if the narrative is long, the egoic brain or conscious mind has become overly involved, overriding the more subtle subconscious mind. This is problematic because it is the subconscious mind from which the messages contained within the dreams are coming. Once the ego gets involved, the messages can become blurred.

Overall, however, what is most important in dream work is simply giving attention to the significance of our dreams. As we do this, our dreams become an extension of our own innate inner healing wisdom. This wisdom is trying to help us complete unfinished business from the day, remind us of something deeper that we are needing to learn, or introduce us to something that has been stored in the subconscious mind and is ready to be addressed. Taking the time to observe and to write notes about our dreams sends a message to the subconscious mind that reinforces that dreams are important. In such, we will be rewarded with more awareness of our dreams. Greater awareness will lead to greater remembering, and as more dreams are remembered, they become clearer and easier to understand.

This is very similar to using the messages or cues we get in our external world as a mirror for what is going on in our internal world. Our energy system draws to itself things of a like vibration so that we can become aware of what we are focusing on or need to focus on. The difference is that in our physical reality, these clues and messages can be quite tangible, while dreams are typically more symbolic. The subconscious mind loves to work with symbols. So again, as we become more aware of them and give them our attention, we also become more familiar with what our subconscious is trying to tell us. Additionally, as we work with our unique symbolic system, we increasingly tune into our innate inner healing wisdom. This wisdom already knows what we need and is trying to guide us into figuring it out.

Understanding to Interpretation -

Now that we've done the foundational work of establishing the purpose and value of our dreams, discussed the various forms they take, and started to consider ways to deduce and work with their meanings, it's time to play with some actual dream interpretation. I've already incorporated a few of my dreams and how I've worked with them into earlier sections. But now we're going to step away from my dreams and into the incredible dream world of my friend, author and artist, Deana Hoover. Deana's dreams are very detailed and highly imaginative. So, as you turn this page, be prepared to be entertained as you enter into the open-hearted subconscious of this warm and talented woman, willing to let us into her dreams.

Chapter Two – Playing with Interpretation

What would a dream book without a dreamer be? It would just be a book about concepts and ideas on the who, what, where, why and when of dreaming. But wow! You add a dreamer and the process becomes organically alive and vibrant, allowing us to enter into the multidimensional consciousness of another. This is akin to a movie or a novel, only with less boundaries and more "stuff."

My dreamer is a dear friend to me. Her name is Deana (pronounced Dee-na) Hoover and she is a talented author and artist. Deana has generously opened her conscious and subconscious to us so that I can help my readers learn to work with their dreams. While I have been helping clients for years to understand and process their own dreams, I asked Deana to be part of this project because her dreams are hilarious to me and I thought it would be fun. In fact, it was while working with Deana's "Talking Dog" dream, which is one of the last dreams we'll be interpreting, that this book became a waking dream for me.

What happened however, in perfect Universal fashion, was that during the time period in which Deana recorded and we subsequently processed her dreams, she was in a significant period of loss. Thus, her dreams were not the usual "Deana" funny. As you know however after reading Chapter One, the Universe knew that it was time to break our hearts open so wide that we could reach within our dreams for healing and truth.

As you read, it is my hope that you will naturally glide into a new awareness of the significance of dreaming and the personal and transpersonal nature of dream interpretation. I also hope that you will be inspired by the healing and humor that raw honesty can bring.

With that said, please join the adventure of dreaming with Deana.

Dream I – Clearing Dream

KYM: Deana, as we start, I want to thank you again for taking the last month or so to record your dreams so that we can share the process of interpretation. You have done an unbelievable job at note taking and journaling. That will make this entire experience richer and more rewarding for all of us. So, before we begin, is there anything that you'd like to share?

DEANA: I just want to say how excited I am to be part of this project. I also want to say how glad I am that we did this when we did. This has been a very intense emotional time for me and I feel that because I was paying such close attention to my dreams, they really helped me release a lot of grief and frustration. I am very grateful to be aware of that and I might not have been if we weren't doing this.

KYM: That is a great point. Awareness is the beginning of emotional growth and healing. Without awareness, things happen to us. With awareness, they happen for us. On that note, let's see what awareness the first dream brings.

38

DEANA: OK. My husband, Scott, and I had some old wooden tools that we loved and used all the time. I think they were bamboo. Anyway, we stored them away, moved on to different things and then we found them again and that made us happy. I don't even know what they were for, but they had a little bit of soil on them as if we had used them in the garden. We put them in the sink to re-hydrate them so that they would be useful again. That was the whole dream.

KYM: So what's been going on with you and Scott?

DEANA: Well, because Scott was recently laid off from his job, I did feel like this dream meant that we were digging up old tools that we used to use. Tools, that we are going to have to reuse and remember how to use because now things are changing and we want to go back to things that had worked in the past.

KYM: Good. The old wooden tools are something that you liked, so when you found them again you could use them. Now, let's consider the re-hydrating. Often when water is present, it represents emotions. Could it be that you are adding a new emotional component to those tools?

DEANA: Yes, absolutely! I feel like we are so much more in touch with our emotions now. We're aware of them and are embracing and honoring them more. It's also been a very emotional time because of our dog, Sadie, dying. The bright side of all the intense emotions is that we have been together a lot and that feels really good.

KYM: Yes, and I remember you saying recently that you've really been loving "hanging out" with your husband.

DEANA: Yes, we have even joked about when it might be time to start "not liking each other." But we have actually really liked spending time together. So, I can definitely see that as emotion that is being infused into the old tools that we liked before and that are still good. But now it almost seems like it's on a more mature level because of how we are processing things.

KYM: Also, the fact that when Scott was working and you were working, you weren't together very much, so you didn't need some of those tools. However, when you're together more constantly you need some of those tools again.

DEANA: Yes. That feels right.

KYM: OK. So now let's look at the overall dream, how did it make you feel?

DEANA: That's a very good question because there was a mix of feelings. While I loved the texture and the quality of the tools, I also felt a tiny bit of nervousness about relying on them because they were old. So it was a mostly happy dream with a bit of nervousness which is exactly the way this feels with Scott losing a job he didn't like. We're pretty happy about it, with a little bit of nervousness.

KYM: Good insight.

DEANA: Wow! You're so good at what you do. Putting it all together like that really makes sense.

Discussion Points: This dream is an example of how we use our dreams to clear stuck energy. There wasn't a lot of charge to it but there was a sense of conflicting feelings that needed to be resolved. What I find to be great about working with this take on Jungian dream interpretation is that it is the dreamer himself that takes the lead in the interpretation by applying it to their life and experiences. I'm just asking questions and making suggestions.

To that end, most of the questions I ask are similar for each dream, and the most important one is, "how did the dream make you feel?" When working with dreams, it's always best to focus on how the dream felt. Because sometimes you can have things that seem one way, like ominous or scary. But if the dream doesn't feel that way, it can be giving you a different message. In this dream, Deana's conflicting feelings of "happy" and "nervous" are good examples of this and were the motivating factors underlying this dream.

Dream 2 – Imagery Dream

KYM: OK, so are we ready for another dream?

DEANA: Yes, let's see…In this dream I wore a wristwatch-like device. You could snap something like a coffee pod into it but it was rectangular. And when you popped the pod in it would result in creating an advertisement to sell your product. I had a product. I had an advertisement for it and the advertisement wasn't very good. The acting was poor and the writing was mediocre.

I didn't know whether I should pop in another pod to get another ad because it felt like kind of a waste of another pod when I already had an ad. I felt very lethargic about my product and about doing anything about it. It all seemed mediocre. The mediocrity of the advertisement seemed to mirror the mediocrity of this product I didn't care much about and I didn't feel like wasting another pod.

At this point, I think I woke up for awhile, dreamed something else briefly, then went back to the same dream.

At that point, I met the advertising executive responsible for the technology of the wrist device. His name was something like Apollo or Zeus. I didn't like that so I took to calling him Pumpkin.

[Laughter]

KYM: I just love how your subconscious works…from a Greek god to a pumpkin.

DEANA: I may have pronounced it "Punkin."

KYM: OK, good. So, let's start out with how the dream made you feel. Part one of the dream, how did it make you feel?

DEANA: Part one felt almost boring. I was not really engaged in anything except for when it came to the second part and I kind of poked at the inventor for his self importance.

KYM: OK. So how did the second part feel?

DEANA: That was hilarious, it amused me.

KYM: Good. So let's look at this, beginning with the first part of the dream. What's been going on in your life right now that feels like you're giving it energy but it's just mediocre?

DEANA: I think it's about work. I'm an artist but recently, because my husband is out of work, I decided to look for a job. However, I have really done nothing about it. I don't want a regular job. But I've been thinking I should put in applications. Then I see the job listings and I'm like, "Hmm, no." So I don't even pick one [application] up. Or I see them online and don't even fill them out. I thought if I have to do something other than create art, I think I just want to clean people's houses.

KYM: So a normal job feels mediocre to you?

DEANA: It really does.

KYM: OK, so the pod, what would it represent in your life right now?

45

DEANA: I think that it represents my energy because it was like a little coffee pod and I was wearing it right where my pulse is.

KYM: Interesting point.

DEANA: I just feel so lethargic about that kind of work.

KYM: And not wanting to use another pod, would that be not wanting to waste any more energy on work you don't want to do?

DEANA: Definitely.

KYM: When you were first telling the dream, it felt like it represented time, which in effect is the same thing. Your time is your energy and visa versa.

DEANA: Yes, I think it is time and energy because it's like a wrist watch but I wore it on the side of my wrist where you take your pulse.

KYM: Good. Did this dream come recently?

DEANA: Yes.

KYM: So it sounds like it is telling you that you're not wanting to waste your time, because it's not just a waste of time and it's mediocre, but it doesn't make you excited. It doesn't feel good.

DEANA: That's exactly how I feel.

KYM: OK, so now let's go to the second part of the dream. You said it felt hilarious and it amused you. So in regard to the first part, in which you equated it to work and using your energy, is there something about that that is funny or amusing?

DEANA: Yes, it is funny and really fits right in because I find it hugely amusing when people have this externally imposed importance. That cracks me up and I want to call them "Punkin."

KYM: So if every part of the dream is you, how is this you? How is Zeus or Apollo and then Punkin, because they're the same, how do they represent a part of you?

DEANA: This is a perfect question. You're so good, because my tummy is telling me this is the key, "Here it is, Punkin." When I do most jobs, I do them well. I learn quickly and become the best one at the job because I can really apply myself. For example, when I worked at the college, everybody told me how good I was and they wanted to invite me to the "important club." But, I never wanted to be in that club because it's funny to me. You're not important because of this thing you do. You're important because of who you are inside. That's just funny whether it comes my way or goes a different direction. It's just funny.

KYM: So who is Zeus or Apollo?

DEANA: They're Gods.

KYM: But who, if they are you, who are they? What part

of you do they represent? Could they be your ego?

DEANA: Yes, I think they would be.

KYM: So here your ego seems to be claiming the status of a God and is full of self importance. Then there's the other part of you that finds humor in that. So it seems that when you think you're too good you find a way to take yourself off the pedestal. You call yourself Punkin or your ego Punkin and it's more human. Does that resonate at all?

DEANA: It does. Because tying back to part one of the dream, I'm realizing I really don't want to do this mediocre thing.

KYM: So I would say that this dream is helping you work through the underlying feelings you have around work and how you use your energy or time. The first is that no, this is not creative for you; it's not a creative expression. There's also a part that deals with thinking you're too good for that. So as you work through that, you use humor to find balance between the gods and Punkin.

DEANA: I think it's funny that I feel that I'm too good to work for the State but not too good to clean people's houses. In fact, I actually like that idea. If I have to do something other than art, I'll go clean people's houses.

KYM: That sounds like humility. "I'm too good to work at the State but I'll clean your house, Punkin."

DEANA: Yeah, and I'm really ready to own my power to choose...although I'd really rather make art.

KYM: Well, I'm pretty sure that if Apollo and Zeus have anything to say about it, you will.

[Laughter}

Discussion Points: The technique that I used when helping Deana work with this dream was an extension of the Jungian philosophy in which each part of the dream reflects something within Deana. As we took the dream apart, I had Deana consider how each significant part showed her something about herself. This requires some deeper reflection and sometimes, as with this dream, I will give suggestions if the dreamer gets stuck, always checking in with them to make sure that we're on the right track.

This is a very useful technique. Frequently when first reviewing a dream, we tend to want to put it outside of ourselves, thinking that we're dreaming about our husbands or a friend or whatever. And while this can be true, it is also true that in our dreams, each one of those aspects can tell us something about ourselves. We just need to ask the question then consider the possibilities.

Dream 3 – Processing Emotions

KYM: Deana, you're doing great. Are you ready for the next dream?

DEANA: I am. This is the most recent of what I am calling my Sadie dreams. Sadie was our precious basset hound and we just had to put her to sleep. I still miss her so much and she's been in my thoughts and dreams a lot.

So, here is the dream. There was a big tank, like a big water tank. It was practically all drained out. So I had to go up on this platform and I put in a hose and start refilling. It was slowly, slowly refilling. This is the part that makes me cry. My little Sadie came and I got to hold her. I still miss her so bad. So I got to just hold her which is what I really, really wanted. She just let me, which is what she would do. I just held her and held her. I was completely aware it was a dream and I just took advantage of holding her. I held her as long as I could.

After I held her for awhile in my hands there was this catalog. It was a very ordinary, mundane kind of catalog that you might get in the mail, something like a Sears catalog. The interesting part was when you turned it over it had a reverse catalog on the other side. That was a Christmas catalog. That was the whole dream. I love her

so much. That was a more...(trying not to cry)

KYM: You can feel it, Deana. Don't rush. (Deana cries for a few minutes then starts again.)

DEANA: I don't think that dream was too much of a challenge to figure out.

KYM: Tell me what you think it means.

DEANA: The big giant water tank of feelings that all drain out, drain out of my eyes. You know, then refilling.

KYM: Refilling?

DEANA: All the emotions empty out and, you know, get a little better. Then you fill the emotions back up. They still kind of drain out and it takes awhile, but you finally get them full again. And then Sadie gave me the chance to hold her because I love her. I just wanted a chance to hold her again and I got that. (Stops for a minute then starts again.)

My feeling with the catalog is like I just figured things will turn around about Christmas time. You might be able to figure more into it than that. But my first instinct was that there would be a turnaround. I've been crying every single day and that might quit because I don't imagine that I will cry every single day until Christmas. I'd turn around the catalog, so that would be turning around my emotions. When you mentioned earlier about using words, I think that would be a turnaround and a timeframe.

KYM: That might be it. But there are two other words that stand out to me, Christmas and reversed. Let's just throw this out there for thought. Christmas time is what? What do you do? What do you get?

DEANA: Typically I don't do much.

KYM: OK. But speaking from a mass consciousness perspective, Christmas is about gifts. So, could this be about gifts? Is there a gift here? Could the point be that there's a gift here for you?

DEANA: Could be.

KYM: When you look at it from a different perspective, reverse it. There's a gift.

DEANA: Yes.

KYM: Deana, besides being an artist you are an author. So, what if this wasn't just a catalog, it was a book? And, if you reverse it and look at it differently, could there be a gift of a new book in this for you?

DEANA: It could be.

KYM: Possibly?

DEANA: It could be. Whether it's specifically about Sadie or...

KYM: Maybe it's about the grieving process and finding the gift.

DEANA: It feels to me like it's layered. On one layer, it could be as simple as time is going to make it feel better. Also, it does seem like layering, like there are more meanings.

KYM: The reason I wouldn't interpret it as time is that the first catalogue had nothing to do with time. You said that it was like a Sears catalog, just something very mundane. And then you reversed it and got Christmas. For me that doesn't feel like it's drawing the parallel with time.

DEANA: I see what you're saying because if it was a planting guide I'd be getting fall, but it's a Christmas tree so I get winter. I see. Yes, the Sears part held zero interest for me. It did feel like the message I connected to was Christmas. That was the significant part. The different perspective and then…

KYM: I know you don't celebrate Christmas in the normal way, how everybody else does. What does Christmas mean to you?

DEANA: I think in a large way it illustrates to me how I do see the world differently than other people. I will look at Christmas and other people and not be able to relate to that at all. So in one way that's it. In some ways I actively don't even like it. In other ways I mean I just don't resonate with it.

KYM: When you turned it over and saw the Christmas tree in the dream, what did you feel like?

DEANA: It did seem pretty. It was a pretty little picture. I have some recollection of what it was, but the thing I looked at in particular was the tree. I thought that it was a pretty Christmas tree. Usually to me they're so tacky, garish, I don't see what people do that for. But every now and then I'll see one I like and that makes sense. This one had the white lights and just looked pretty. It was just a passing thought. Hmmm, why don't I like Christmas? I just don't.

KYM: What do you feel about trees? Because what you specifically noticed was the tree.

DEANA: I do love trees.

KYM: If you were to think about what trees mean to you, what do you come up with?

DEANA: Life and growth and I believe that's what they mean at Christmas time too. There's also a turnaround because that's the solstice and now the days will start getting longer and things will come back to life, as it were. Plus they smell good.

KYM: You just said it. They mean growth, they mean life, and this is part of the cycle of life. Losing your pet, your little Sadie, is part of the cycle of life.

DEANA: I have thought before about the cut down Christmas tree. You know, you kill the tree that represents life.

KYM: So could that be why you saw a Christmas tree?

DEANA: Yes because that was the end of Sadie. Plus we did it. We chose it for her.

KYM: So if this is your subconscious mind's way of sending you a message about that, what do you think it's saying?

DEANA: Well, you know, it was the end of her life and we picked it but we just picked the time because it was time. But life goes on. I mean the larger cycle of life goes on. Things continue. Things turn around and you grow.

KYM: And Christmas also represents a season and this was that season or cycle for you.

DEANA: Yes. Again, things turnaround, yes.

KYM: So the important thing to realize too, when you're looking at dreams, is that they are multifaceted. You've used the word "layers" a couple times with this dream. One layer is that our dreams can allow us to process unfinished business or unfelt or overwhelming emotions. You are processing, and Sadie was helping you process, a lot of emotion around the loss, the grief that you were feeling about her being gone.

Another layer, which is really a great thing about dreams, is that they transcend concrete reality. In that reality, Sadie is gone. But in dream consciousness Sadie's really not gone. On some level she is still here with you, and on that level you got to hold her. In that way, dreams can take us out of our linear view of time and space and into all time and space. They can help us traverse this thing that we think is so real and allow us to tap into consciousness and connection that is far more real.

DEANA: That's very appropriate for this dream in particular because in our lives we're in this wavelength tied to this timeline. This is where we feel it and live it and exist even if we know it's bigger than that. We can tap into the other side but still, this is where we are and this is where we need to process. It's just so awesome though to have these magical dreams that aren't limited by that.

KYM: True. And, in the moment of our dream, the dream is as much reality as our waking state is.

DEANA: Yes. And I got to hold my dog.

KYM: And you got to hold your dog and you can do that again in your dreamtime.

Deana: Yes.

KYM: And you'll be able to do it without the sadness. Right now it's still about the grief. But as you work through it, it gets to be more about the joy and the celebration.

DEANA: You're right. In the beginning it was just only being torn apart. But even now I'm starting to remember things she used to do and I know that it will be funny again. I'm looking forward to spending time with her and having it be the celebration part too because she was a great dog. She deserves to have, deserves to be, the whole thing, all the happy and the sad and all of it.

KYM: I think you and Sadie, just like people, had a soul contract. She came and brought you all the wonderful things that she brought to your life as part of the contract. She also brought you the grief and loss as part of the contract too so that you can learn to feel this deeply with a being that you loved so unconditionally.

DEANA: I feel that way too.

KYM: Where some of the other losses that you've had in your life have almost been a relief, the loss of Sadie is allowing you to feel those feelings with someone that you love so much.

DEANA: You said that very well because even in the beginning I was aware that this feels like healthy grief. You know, when my mother died it was a relief. When my dad died, it was weird and complicated. I felt like we were never going to be able to make things right. But with Sadie, I thought, "So this is what healthy grief feels like. It's better." Really, if you have to feel grief, I pick this one, healthy.

KYM: That's such a great way to look at this, because when you can feel your feelings without stuffing them or avoiding them, you can heal them. And there's no unfinished business.

DEANA: Right, so that was clearly part of it, allowing myself to feel healthy grief. Sadie, my little treasure girl in so many ways.

Discussion Points: In this section, we've talked about the layers of the dream and have illustrated the value of going beyond face value. For example, while Deana had initially thought that Christmas in her dream meant time, with deeper evaluation, it became clear that it was more about growth and life, and cycles and seasons, as represented symbolically by the tree.

Something else that is useful to note is that we discussed several hypotheses before landing on the one that felt the best and most accurate for Deana because of her unique view of Christmas. Based on my worldview of Christmas and gift giving, I suggested that the gift being given might be the subject for a book about Deana's healthy grieving process. When that didn't resonate with her, we kept digging and ultimately found the key that helped bring the dream into a clearer focus. That key was the tree.

This reinforces the value of creating a personal dream dictionary. Further, it not only applies to the tree and what trees symbolize to Deana, which was very significant in finding the deeper meaning of this dream, but also to Christmas. While the tree was the key symbol, Christmas was the first entry point and meant something very different to the dreamer than it did to me, the interpreter. Had we stayed with either of our first thoughts, we would not have looked further to find the key element.

Dream 4 – Working Through the Layers

DEANA: I find that as we go through these dreams, I like referring back to the notes and spending a moment remembering the dream because then the visual and essence of it comes back.

KYM: When you say essence, it sounds like your referring to overall feeling of the dream is that right?

DEANA: Yes, the feeling and the story.

KYM: OK good, let's start.

DEANA: This was another layered dream and part of it was deeply emotional. There was that same thread of stress and a little discomfort that shows up in some of the other dreams we've just talked about. It was also a dream that was hitting on an intellectual level.

We lived on this slope of a mountain. This mountain wasn't my usual dream mountain. It was more like foothills. It's an ensemble dream. The people kind of faded in and out of being different people. We lived in a group. There were all these different groups and different houses. It came to my mind, so I'm sure this is significant, the house that we lived in, the paint had all faded to gray, a dark gray. We were building a fire, a cooking fire outside of the house.

The person that was with me sort of morphed in and out of being my husband, Scott. Until the end of the dream he was the only one that ever became a real person. Everybody else was sort of like extras and ensemble cast.

So we were building a cooking fire. We were using these big square construction logs that we had cut up. He had half covered them in plastic, long ways, in order to slow the rate of burn and to protect them from getting dirty from the cooking fat.

I was a little concerned because the vapors from plastic would get into the food. This was a little bit of a discussion. We cooked whatever it was. We put out the fire. Then I was pulling the logs out to save them so that we would continue to be able to use them as long as possible. I pulled the plastic off the logs and not only did they not have any fat spilled on them, but they were completely unburned; not even scorched. I felt very fortunate about this because our concern (we had a double concern with this) is that we just knew we did not have enough firewood to last us for the winter. Winter was coming on. We simply didn't have enough. We figured we'd cross that bridge when we came to it.

At the same time, within our household family group, someone had died. What we wanted to do, and that was part of our cultural healing, is to build a big bonfire to release them. We absolutely didn't have enough wood to build the bonfire and to get through the winter, to get comfortably through winter. I was about to say survive the winter. We didn't have any doubt we would survive the winter. It would just be cold and we didn't know how that would happen. But on this mountain and in this community you had to build a bonfire and you had to file paper work to do so.

Within seven days of the death you could, for the culture, build the bonfire and have a ceremony and cry and whatever else to release the person. Then that was part of the healing process. Six and a half days after we filled out the paper work and saw the sun was setting, we knew we weren't getting permission. If you did it anyway, if you built the bonfire without permission, everybody would see it and the government would come and they would break up your group and you would all be scattered about. You didn't know who you would be with. We liked our group and didn't want to be split up.

We, as a group, decided to find our own way to heal rather than break the bonfire law. We were trying to figure out what that was. So we were all standing around talking about it and we put aside our wood. We thought, "On the bright side, our wood will last a little bit longer." But now we were going to have to figure out our own way to do this.

Right about then, we were so proud because this feeling, this wonderful feeling, came when music started coming out of the house. The person that was still in the house, who wouldn't come out here to talk with us, was our person in the group who had Down's Syndrome. He figured out how to play music with this old record player that was kind of jerry-rigged. He didn't know how to work it, but figured it out. And so we were so proud that he figured it out and that music was coming out of the house, out to this little yard where we're all standing. At this point, we were just enjoying the music and were glad we were going to figure this out.

The dream sort of started changing into another dream at

this point because someone in the group was taking care of the baby animals in the barn. They sort of morphed too and there were different animals. Then the dream shifted. It was the Cosby house and Felicia Rashaad, the mom from the Cosby's, made some remarks. Now we realized that the baby animals in the barn were baby ducks. Mrs. Cosby made some more remarks. The baby ducks were there and everybody thought it was a secret. They didn't know the baby ducks were there but she was so smart. She is the Cosby mom, she is onto everything. Hahaha, she knew ducks were there all along. That was the whole dream.

KYM: (Laughing) I love the ending and the way that your subconscious brought it all together. So, what do you think it's about?

DEANA: There's so much of that dream that's beyond me. I feel like the fact it's on the foothills is significant because many of my mountain dreams have so much meaning to me. The death in the group is obviously representative of Sadie because she was the death in our group, maybe. I also key into that we couldn't mourn in the traditional way. We had to figure it out our own way. We wanted to keep together what we had because we liked it. There's so much about it that it's like...I don't know.

KYM: I will drop the bomb, okay? I think it's a sex dream.

DEANA: Okay. [Laughter] Tell me how.

KYM: All right. To start, any time you have a dream that has a house in it, it's about you. You are the house. So what first started triggering me, suggesting that this is a sex dream, is that the colors of the house were faded and gray, dark gray, which is kind of dreary. And you make the point that it has changed in some way. This tells me that you might be feeling like something about you has changed and become dreary.

Next you start talking about fire. In a dream, fire may represent anger, but it can also represent passion. In this case, there didn't seem to be anger in your discussion, what you were concerned about was that Scott had put plastic on the logs to slow down the fire. So it feels to me like there may have been some concern that you weren't as passionate about each other. You're best friends and you enjoy living together, but some part of you may be concerned about a slowing or lack of passion.

DEANA: Well, you know, there definitely has been a drop off as we have gotten older. We used to be like monkeys. [Laughter]

KYM: Has that been a concern at all for you? In your conscious mind?

DEANA: Mildly. You know, it's not a big pressing thing but every now and then it will cross my mind.

KYM: So there are a couple things that happen. I'm really glad that you told me this dream and that it was so long, so seemingly complicated because what it feels like to me is that this was just your subconscious mind working something out. You talked about houses and people living in groups, in different houses. To me, these represent thoughts. These are your thoughts, bunches of thoughts. So then you get to your house, the house that's you, and you create this story.

What it feels like to me by the end of the dream, is that the whole thing was about working that out. You needed to find your own way to make this make sense, to work it out, and so in comes the part of you that is reflected in the Down's Syndrome person. I believe this is the part of you that may seem disabled to the outside world, but to the inside world (inside the house) it is the part that thinks differently and therefore finds a solution that makes you feel good.

By the end of it you've created this long story to work through the concern and when it gets resolved it's funny. Just like the Apollo Zeus dream. You do this when Mrs. Cosby finds the ducks. You pull it all around at the end and tie a bow on it. You get your ducks in order so to speak.

DEANA: The idea of the thoughts really works for me

because at one point I sort of wondered what the government would be. I guess it would be your higher reasoning that would be making the rules.

KYM: Making the rules?

DEANA: Yes. The part that's making the rules doesn't care about how you feel. It's a rule so you have to do it and your feelings just have to work themselves out.

KYM: That's why in this dream I'm not sure that the person that died is Sadie. It feels like there is a part of you that has died, possibly that younger you that used to "do it" like monkeys. That part of you is gone but you still found a way to celebrate that.

DEANA: Yes, the music comes through the window. I liked that part. That part completely resonates. We're all standing outside talking about how we're going to fix this problem, and when we go farther in, it's the one who is theoretically damaged who figures it out without trying. We're going to play music!

KYM: And why does playing music seem so right?

DEANA: I think it's because music is tapped into feelings.

KYM: And, you didn't think about it.

DEANA: Right. Once we hear the music we just know that it is right and we don't need to figure it out. It just happens.

KYM: So, there's nothing to worry about, the problem will solve itself naturally.

DEANA: Yes! That feels right.

Discussion Points: When working with this dream, I did more direct interpretation than I normally do. I did this because I could sense that Deana was getting bogged down by the length and elaborate telling of the story. So, I dropped in my initial intuitive hit to see how it resonated, and it seemed to. Additionally, as we talked about the possibilities, it became clear that this dream wasn't so much about the details but was more Deana's way of allowing her mind to work something out.

This illustrates how different dreams serve different purposes at different times. As we move through these dreams, we start to see how therapeutic dreamtime can be, such as in the dream with Sadie in which deep emotions were being processed. Whereas in this dream it wasn't really so much about the emotions as it was working it out in the thoughts. And then for Deana, because she thinks in stories with characters and plots, it took her some shifts in the plot to get it all worked out in her subconscious mind. Once it did, there was resolution and humor. So part of the value of our dreams is that they help us work out unresolved issues, some as simple as something unprocessed from the day, and some more complicated, nagging or obscured from the conscious waking mind.

There's another point I'd like to make. When helping Deana work through this dream, she had written a lot of notes. That is good. However, as a general rule, when I'm working with someone, even when I'm working with my own dreams, I encourage the dreamer to just write down key things that come up in the dream. For example in this dream I might have written gray house, logs that are wrapped in plastic, fire, seven day rule, or whatever. It can be good to write longer narratives, but as I've mentioned before, that can get in the way. First, people may not be consistent in taking the time to record the dream and second, the egoic mind starts to take over.

This being said, I discussed this with Deana and she indicated that she needed the notes to remember. In this case, Deana knows her own processing and what works best for her. This is a great awareness. For all dreamers, it is important to find the way that works for you. That way, you're more apt to stay with the practice. And, again, the more attention you give to your dreams, the more they're going to give to you.

Chapter Three – Re-Scripting

Do you remember when you were a child and you had a bad dream? You'd wake your mom or dad up and they would tell you to go back to bed and think about something that you liked. For me it was a field of wildflowers. Anyway, in a sense, they were having you do a modified version of what I call re-scripting.

By redirecting your thinking from something that was scary or frustrating to something more pleasant, you were able to calm your mind and go back to sleep. The difference, however, is that with re-scripting, you intentionally complete an incomplete dream, or one that is not to your liking, with a new more desirable ending or outcome.

This works because when the body/mind is in a deeply relaxed state, the subconscious mind opens and becomes receptive. Therefore, the secret to using this technique is to first decide how you would have liked the dream to end. Then close your eyes, breathe deeply, relax and imagine the dream as you would have liked it to be. Make sure to include details and feelings that will help make it more real for you.

This is a very effective technique for two reasons. The first is that it can help to release the energy of a negatively charged dream so that you don't carry that feeling into your day. The second, as you will see below, is that it can be the beginning of breaking the pattern of incompletion or dissatisfaction that was at the core of the dream.

Dream 5 – Re-Scripting for Resolution

DEANA: I had an art show at a coffee shop, similar to one I like to go to. I'm all set and ready to go. The venue is ready. I'm ready. I go out to my vehicle to get my art and I start bringing it in. Suddenly the path is blocked, hugely blocked. There's a big black grand piano sitting right in the way and at the key board is this big man in his big black suit. On top of the piano keyboard he has his computer keyboard and he's working on his computer. I'm standing there with my art and thinking, "I don't know what to do. I could easily ask him to move. He won't care. But I can't get my art past the piano." Now I'm really frustrated. The dream ended with me trying to figure out a way around this block that's stopping me from getting to my really great art show.

KYM: So, as you remember the dream, how did it feel?

DEANA: The beginning of the dream felt like a feeling that I get when I do an art show. It's a very specific feeling but I'm not sure how to name it. It has some anticipation in it as well as a feeling of readiness, like I'm in the zone. But the minute I walked up and found that my way was blocked, the feeling went to frustration, huge frustration.

KYM: And how did you feel when you woke up? Was the frustration still there?

DEANA: Not to the degree it was in the dream. You

know how sometimes your dream feelings just hang on? Well when I woke up I was kind of relieved because I didn't have to figure out how to get past the piano.

KYM: So after feeling like you were in the zone, you felt blocked and frustrated. Right?

DEANA: That's right.

KYM: If you were to think of that feeling, is there something in your waking life that has you feeling a similar feeling of being blocked and frustrated?

DEANA: The thing in real life that compares to that feeling is the repeated blocks around my art. I've had a lifetime of just wanting to do the art and fulfill the dream but not being able to for so many reasons. First you have little kids, you have to put food on the table, you have to get the regular job, and you have to be responsible. Now comes the kid with the drug addiction, then comes the kid with the mental health problems, then comes the trying to just pay the bills. I mean all the big and little things that come along. And now, your husband loses his job and you might need to get one. Damn it! Move the fricking piano already! I'm going to burn down the piano. The frustration keeps building. Lately I've noticed that even if a small thing gets in my way, the frustration comes quickly because of all the times I've told myself, "It will be cool, it will be cool, we'll make it right." But I don't want to make it right. I don't want to wait for the next thing. I don't want to be patient. I'm ready!

KYM: Okay. Let's close your eyes and get into the dream. Here you are, all loaded up with your art.

DEANA: Okay.

KYM: You're loaded up with your art and you encounter the piano. You see the big man in his big black suit. And, you just can't get buy. Now I want you to use your imagination to create a new ending to the dream, to finish it any way you want.

DEANA: [Pause] Ahh, that's nice.

KYM: Finish it, feel it. Feel it deep inside yourself. Feel yourself moving around the piano, however you do it, whatever way is right, you know how to do it. You can do it. You have all the resources you need and I want you to get on the other side of the piano. I want you to set your art out, hang it.

DEANA: I like that.

KYM: Yes. Somehow, maybe with the help of the man, move the piano to the side so everybody can get in and see your art. Ask for help, it's okay to ask for help.

DEANA: There came the funny ending.

KYM: All right. Give us the funny ending.

DEANA: Okay. So I went in and I used dream magic, so I didn't have to put my paintings down. They stayed with me because I'm not leaving them behind again. Then I shoved the piano out of my way, but that's not good enough. I squeezed it so it got small, squeezed it and squeezed it. Then I used dream magic to hang up my paintings. When I shoved the piano and conquered it with my big dream muscles I got a really cool feeling that reminded me of a reoccurring dream I used to have when I was a kid.

I used to dream regularly of being killed by dogs, being left out on the Siberian tundra, left for the pack of dogs to eat while the family kept going. It was very graphic. The dogs would come into my dreams in other places too. But when I was 13 years old I got pissed and started killing the dogs with my bare hands and never dreamt of them after that. Moving the piano had that same power. First I shoved it out of my way and then squeezed it until it was little. I felt like Superman! Then, as I turned around and looked at the man, he was laughing. He was like, "It's cool, I got it," and he started playing this tiny piano. [Laughter] It was like Linus. He thought it was funny. He was like, "I'm playing a tiny piano for your art reception."

[Laughter]

Discussion Points: What Deana just did was find resolution to the frustrations that she was processing in her dream by creating a new ending. In this case, she found a humorous way to release the tension and find completion. This is especially useful when a dream just doesn't feel finished. You go back to the dream and imagine how you would have liked it to go and allow yourself to replace the feelings of frustration, or whatever, with feelings that are more satisfactory. In that way, it is the desired outcome that brings resolution to both the feelings and the dream.

Further Processing:

KYM: How do you feel after creating this new ending?

DEANA: I feel relief and lighter.

KYM: Good. So, the dream provided the opportunity to acknowledge feelings, old limiting beliefs and patterns. The dream brought up the real-time feelings of frustration around not being able to do your art. This was supported by the limiting belief that there's always going to be something in your way. And the pattern is that you give up before finding a way or asking for help. But now, by using your imagination to recreate the ending you shift the frustration with humor. In doing this, you are telling your subconscious mind that, not only is it okay to remove the blocks, it can actually be empowering and fun. And, what's wonderful about the subconscious mind is that it doesn't know the difference between what's real and what's imagined. Or in this case, what was in the actual dream and what you made up.

DEANA: It's so cool because I really feel like I don't have to keep just finding my way around things. I can actually remove the blocks. I'm so ready for that! It's kind of like walking around with a middle finger to anything that wants to be in my way.

KYM: Sounds empowering.

DEANA: And feels great!

Dream 6 – Re-Scripting for Clearing

DEANA: So my husband, Scott, was driving the car home. For some reason I wanted to save gas and not ride in the car. Even at the time I think I had a little trouble trying to make that logical, but that was what was happening. While I walked, it started to get colder so I had to take my stuff out of the car to bundle up. Then I went to Starbucks so that I would have a hot coffee on my way home. I remember feeling a little bit of frustration about having to walk home even though I had made that choice.

KYM: Is that the entire dream?

DEANA: Yes and I woke up feeling frustrated and irritated.

KYM: OK. What do you think the dream means?

DEANA: That Scott, maybe it's easy for him. I don't really think that's true. I have had similar dreams to this before. They always frustrate me and irritate me a little bit. I think that it's just that I do take a more complicated road and maybe I just needed to feel the feeling.

KYM: Has there been anything in your current waking life that has been frustrating you or irritating you that you might not have acknowledged or felt fully?

DEANA: Nothing big really, but it seems like there have been a lot of little things. And some of them have been my creation.

KYM: Yes, like you choosing to walk when you could ride. You create the situation that creates the frustration.

DEANA: I get it. It's not that complicated. I just need to feel it.

KYM: That is my sense too. I think this dream is helping you realize how you choose the things that make you feel frustrated. For example, in dream language, a car might represent how we move to or through things. In this case you decided to walk home, which took you out of the car and slowed you down. That created frustration.

DEANA: Yes. Every time I have had variations on this dream, that's always what it's about. It's slower.

KYM: Dreams like this one are really cathartic because they help us to process feelings that went unprocessed in the day or days prior to the dream. The feelings are still in us, but need a way to express or work themselves out.

DEANA: So, if I feel my feelings throughout the day, I don't have to have the dream.

KYM: You might still have the dream as a way of processing the feeling on another level.

DEANA: If I can recognize it I can process it differently even in the dream.

KYM: Yes.

DEANA: Instead of just being irritated and do it anyway.

KYM: Additionally, dreams like this can provide the opportunity to intentionally bring the dream to a desirable completion by imagining a new ending. For example, you could have stayed in the car with Scott and just let him drive you home.

DEANA: Or drive the car myself, or fly. I want to fly.

KYM: You could fly, but sometimes it might be worth taking the car rather than flying just because it's part of doing the process. Flying implies circumventing the process, where walking home means making it longer. Just staying in the car might be a way of naturally completing what has been set into motion.

DEANA: I've been getting that message a lot lately but I keep wanting it to be different.

KYM: And when you want it to be different or faster than it is, what happens?

DEANA: OK, I get it. I get more frustrated.

KYM: Yes. So, what would be the equivalent in your waking reality to staying in the car?

DEANA: I guess that it would be to just keep at it and trust that I'll get there when I get there.

KYM: OK, let's test that out. Close your eyes and imagine that you got in the car and let Scott drive you home. Imagine how that feels and what comes next....

DEANA: Oh, you're tricky. When I stay in the car, Scott and I get home in time for a delicious dinner and I feel warm and satisfied instead of cold and frustrated. And I like that way better.

KYM: Good. When you get that it is you making the choices that create both the positive and the negative feelings, that is the beginning to getting where you want to go. Does that feel complete?

DEANA: Yes, it really does. It also makes me hungry.

[Laughter]

Discussion Points: Again in this dream, Deana is working through feelings of frustration. However, they are born out of her choices and she is being challenged to shift a pattern that is keeping her stuck. She realizes this is a pattern and that she is being called to feel her feelings. Additionally, I have her go a step beyond that realization and re-script the ending by making a new choice and feeling the resulting pleasurable outcome. In this way, the subconscious mind starts to work with the new belief that says, "I can make choices that make me feel good," versus the old belief that says "I make choices that cause me frustration."

Chapter Four – Re-Dreaming

In this section, I will be walking Deana through a process that I call re-dreaming. It is basically a hypnotic technique that helps the dreamer re-enter the dream, almost as if she is actually having the dream again. I have found this to be a very useful practice when the dream doesn't seem to be telling you much or when you're having a difficult time remembering the dream. In relaxing the conscious body/mind, the subconscious mind is more accessible and thus the dream itself is more accessible. Additionally, as you will see below, it can help the dreamer to zero in on details that may have been forgotten or even missed in the original retelling.

On to the Dream:

DEANA: The next one is quick and I really love it! OK, here goes. Somebody found a device that searches for life forms like cats and they were demonstrating how to find a cat with it. They're walking around the neighborhood with this device looking for cats and I tell them that I already have one of those devices. You just go, "Here kitty, kitty, kitty." That's the whole dream and even when I was dreaming I thought it was hilarious.

KYM: I love it! Since this is a quick dream and it seems pretty straight forward, I'd like to have you try a technique that I call re-dreaming. It can help you to focus in and notice details that you might not have remembered simply from your notes. Is that OK?

DEANA: Sure. Go ahead.

KYM: OK, so I want you to lean back and relax. Close your eyes and take a deep relaxing breath, exhaling fully. Now take another breath, let your shoulders drop, and as you exhale, feel yourself settling into the chair. Now, take another deep breath and image that your mind is clear and open for the dream that you'll be remembering. Just show me by nodding your head when your mind is clear and ready for the dream. [Deana nods.] Good. Now I'm going to count from one to three and when I reach three, you will be back in the dream as vividly as you dreamed it the first time. Here we go. One, two, three....you're there, you're back in the dream, experiencing it again. Experience the dream fully and completely with heightened awareness. And, when you feel complete, open your eyes and we'll discuss it. [Deana is silent for 3-4 minutes and then takes a breath and opens her eyes.]

KYM: OK. So how was that? Did you notice anything that you hadn't remembered in the first re-telling?

DEANA: I did. I actually remember seeing a cat when I said, "Here kitty, kitty." It was kind of little and fluffy. It was under a bush.

KYM: That's good, you weren't just looking for a cat to be funny, you actually found one. So, what do cats mean to you?

DEANA: Well, they are sweet, independent. I need a

word for this feeling that I have about cats. I just really like them. They seem more like your favorite roommate than your dog. Your dog feels like your kid, your child. Cat seems like your absolute favorite roommate you love hanging out with.

KYM: If you were calling a favorite roommate, what would you be calling a favorite roommate for?

DEANA: Probably to hang out and have fun.

KYM: Okay. And how would you normally call a roommate?

DEANA: I guess I would use a telephone.

KYM: Have you lost your phone?

DEANA: That was awhile ago.

KYM: Misplaced your phone?

DEANA: I'm always setting it aside. I never really know where it is. But it does occur to me that quite often the people that I want to hang out with are the people that are in close proximity because they're right there.

KYM: They're there, it's easy.

DEANA: Yes.

KYM: Okay. I want to throw another twist into what this dream might mean. Are you familiar with archetypes? Archetypes are symbols that have a collectively inherent meaning within the psyche of humankind. The meaning will be similar and understood by all people. It's not so much about the society or the family that you're raised in; it's more encompassing and universal. Cats are archetypically feminine. They represent the feminine and the psychic inner world. That's why they are frequently featured as "familiars" and accompany witches. They help to clear psychic energy, whereas dogs are more masculine, "man's best friend," and help to clear physical energy. So if in this dream someone is coming up with a device to call out the feminine, psychic or something on the psychic realm, and all you have to do is say, "Here kitty, kitty," what else might this dream mean?

DEANA: That all I have to do is open to my psychic abilities and they are waiting right there.

KYM: Does that feel right for you?

DEANA: That seems to match the waking world that has tried to give me a cat for the past two years until finally I went ahead and brought one home.

KYM: The physical world mirroring the inner world, yes.

DEANA: It's like the Universe saying, "Pay attention to this Deana!"

KYM: Yes.

DEANA: Once I took the cat home, people quit trying to give me a cat. So apparently I just have to open the door, let it in, or be mindful of it, I suppose.

KYM: And while many people need a device or some kind of assistance to help them communicate with the transpersonal world, it's easy for you.

DEANA: That is an excellent analogy because I actually laugh. I don't mean to, but I do laugh at some of the "woo woo" stuff people do in order to try to make those connections. I'm like, "Come on, you just do it." You don't have to burn sage and chant, hold hands and sing the song. You just do it.

KYM: So that feels real for you?

DEANA: It really does and it always surprises me when a cute little fun dream like this one turns out to be so much deeper.

KYM: Yes, because our dreams are our subconscious mind communicating with us. And because we each have our own symbolic language we get imagery that we can understand. Your dreams and images are frequently funny because that's how your subconscious is tricking you into listening to something serious, planting the seed of something deeper.

DEANA: Could be, because I do like funny stuff and I know that I've been a bit resistant to really tapping into my psychic gifts. I guess I might want to start working with that.

KYM: So, in regard to the process of doing the re-dreaming, how did that feel going back in?

DEANA: It was good because it really emphasized the cat. It was there peeking out from under a bush and it was fluffy and cute. It's like my unconscious mind was showing me that part of me that is cute, but is hiding.

KYM: When you re-dreamed it, how did you feel when you saw the little hiding cat?

DEANA: I felt like I wanted to reach down and pick it up.

But I was too busy being hilarious.

KYM: Hmmm, something else to be aware of then might be how you choose humor over your other gifts.

DEANA: That is probably true. I'm always fascinated about that. A dream knows exactly where you need to go whether it's complicated or simple.

KYM: That's true, and it's powerful because it's all part of you.

Discussion Points: While this dream was short and Deana focused on the hilarity of it, I had a sense that there was more happening under the surface. So I had her use my re-dreaming technique with the intention of gaining a deeper awareness or heightened memory of the dream. From that exercise, there was a two part message. First was the simplicity of tapping into her psychic gifts and that all she has to do is call upon them. The next, and possibly even more important, is how she relies on humor in deference to her other gifts and talents. Both of these provide Deana with something to be aware of and work with.

Another important point brought out in the discussion of this dream is landing on the right dream language to get to the heart of this dream. I started with looking at Deana's personal meaning for cats but that didn't really seem to lead anywhere. That is when I suggested a more archetypal meaning and that seemed to hit home. Therefore it would be valuable to list both the personal and the archetypal meanings for "cat" in Deana's dream dictionary for future reference in other dreams.

Chapter Five - "The Talking Dog"

As I mentioned in Chapter One, "The Talking Dog" dream is what prompted me to enlist Deana as my dreamer for this book. Her incredible imagination, attention to detail, and ability to retell the story is amazing to me. I delight in it so I know most of you will too.

However, having said that, this dream is quite complicated. It's easy to get sidetracked if you focus on any singular detail. It can also be overwhelming if you look at it as a whole. Therefore, I encourage you to pay attention to the methodical approach that I take. It is the same that I use whether the dream is complicated or simple. Step by step, I ask questions that bring the various aspects of the dream back to Deana. And, it is her answers that lead us to the heart of this whimsical, yet powerful dream.

On to the Dream

DEANA: Okay, so the talking dog. I believe this was the dream that made you and I clearly talk about dreams. Anyway, the dream started where I was in my studio with my friend, Debbie, and there had been an event. She was really helping me clean out and put things back together. She put some strange cushions on the love seat, cushions I had never seen before. I said, "Where did you get these cushions?" She said they were the ones in the back. I thought that was odd and I went to get the right cushions. When I went into the back room looking for the cushions, I discovered a doorway that I'd never noticed before. So of course I had to go see what was on the other side of the door.

I opened the door and I discovered there was a whole world out there, a world different than our world. First, all of the people there were really tall and thin, except that their bellies were distended. They were all wearing the same kind of clothes with long sleeves, long pants, long wool overcoats, and bowler hats. Plus, each person was just one pastel color.

I stepped out onto this platform, a train platform that my door had opened onto. I wanted to go explore this world but I also wanted to get back in. There was no door knob on the outside of the door so I put something in the doorway and propped it open. At this point I became a 10 year old boy who was partly 10 year old boy, partly me.

I stepped out onto the platform and I was kind of watching what was going on. It was a sunny pleasant day and the people were just wandering up and down the street. Well, they didn't really wander. They actually hurried, but were going up and down the street. Busy. They didn't interact very much. They didn't talk to each other. They just hurried to their destination, except when they saw a dog. Then they went to interact with the dogs in great ways. They gushed over the dogs and the dogs talked. Of course, this thrilled me.

The dogs talked to them and were very joyful and wise and wonderful. And they gushed and cooed and fawned over these dogs. And the dogs cheerfully and happily talked to them and they petted the dogs. Then they went on their way and the dogs continued along. Soon they weren't talking to the dogs and they went back to being fairly non-responsive.

I thought, "I have got to get me one of them talking dogs." So I got down off the platform and I went through their little town. It was interesting that all of the buildings were also one pastel color with no other adornments. The sidewalks were wide and bright with sunshine and I was kind of wandering around looking to see how I might kipe (steal) a dog.

I had a memory that would be the little boy's memory of once encountering a talking dog before and thinking, "Oh, this must be where that dog came from." And as far as I can tell they were all strays because they didn't have collars and tags, but the people really loved all of them. And somehow I knew that in a little while another dog would come by.

In the midst of all of this, I saw this sight of a man. The streets and everything else were clean and orderly but the man was lying on the sidewalk suffering. His belly had grown so enormous that he had burst out of his clothes and his body was seething and churning, and he had pig nipples. His face was partly like their faces and also partly like a pig. He was in agony and his eyes were crazy. He was clearly suffering and they didn't acknowledge him in any way. I certainly had never encountered anything like it before. I didn't know what to do so I continued on my little quest for a dog.

Then I saw a dog. He was talking to a little group and they were doing their customary fawning over him. The group went one way and the dog headed another. I thought, "This is perfect, I'll just grab this dog." So I went and picked up the dog and I asked him if he wanted to go with me. And he was happy to do whatever. He was game for anything. So I petted him and loved on him, pretty much fawned on him the way they did. Then I said that I was going to take him home with me and he was fine with that.

On the way back to the platform, I saw the man on the

sidewalk but I just tried to ignore him because I didn't know what else to do. I went past him and I could see the platform and the door, which was now closed. I remembered there was no knob and I now saw that my building looked like a warehouse. I wasn't at all worried because I could clearly see that the train came into that space and occupied the exact same space as the building that I was trying to enter. The doorway overlapped and so I knew what to do. I could just wait for the train to pull up and I then go into the train doorway and out the other side. Then I would be back home. All the while I was just loving on this dog and having such a great time.

So, I went straight through the train and ended up in my house, which was the little boy's house. I got there and everybody was getting ready for a party. One of my friends was having a birthday party and people were starting to arrive. I called my best friend who was a little girl my age named Jessica or Jennifer or something like that. I told her that she had to come see what I had!

She came over and we both started fawning over the little

dog. We were so excited and were trying to decide who we should tell. Suddenly it occurred to me that I hadn't been careful about taking this dog! I was visible out on the street. I was visibly different, none of them responded to me, but I didn't know if they knew I was there. And I knew that I walked right through a train full of people from the other land. I also knew that I had not done anything to conceal the fact that I had taken this dog. And I wondered if they would come for him. I loved the dog already and I didn't want to lose him. So we were trying to make a plan.

At this point our house was filling up with parents and kids, and there was a party in the kitchen with a big cake. We were in the back of the house going, "What are we going to do? Should we even show our friends?" We knew that if we did, there would be more people that knew about the dog. I really loved it and didn't want to be parted from it. I didn't know what to do.

Then my friend asked me what the people from the other land looked like. She nodded toward a mirror. I looked in the mirror and there were three of those men in those pastel color outfits with the bowler hats. But they were different because they didn't have the benign non-recognition on their faces. They were angry and we started talking through the mirror.

They accused me of taking a dog. I told them that I just loved the dog and didn't mean any harm. They said that didn't matter, that these dogs were their gods and I'd taken one of their gods! They told me it was probably too late, that I'd already ruined him. I pled with them saying, "I didn't ruin him! I didn't do anything to him!" Then I started to notice that the dog was talking a little bit less, and a little bit less, and a little bit less. He was losing his ability to communicate.

They told me again that it was too late and I asked what if I brought him back if he'd be able to talk again. They said, "No, you turned him into one of your dogs and our revenge is already exacted upon you. The destruction in your world is already unleashed. You did it and it's what your people deserve!" Then they told me that the destruction would be with fleas. I asked them what I could do and they said there was nothing. They said that I didn't have immunity to this and 75% of our population would succumb. I was stunned and thought, "I don't know what I have done."

I went out to the party and I saw that the people at the party had distended bellies. I went to ask my dad what to do. He was starting to gather the affected ones, mostly children, into the kitchen. He told me that I didn't want to see this and to get out of the room. I asked him what I didn't want to see and what was going to happen. He told me they were going to turn into pig people, they were going to give birth to pig children, and they would not be fully formed. He kept telling me that I didn't want to see it.

At that time one of the kids started getting larger and larger, and started to absorb the other children until there was only one last child. He was huge, just like the man on the street. He was bursting out of his clothing, lying on the ground; the very same way except for the face was half pig, half human now. His belly was churning and I knew that these half-pig, half-human fetuses were in there and that I'd unleashed this. The fleas were already in the world and there was nothing to be done. That's where the dream ends.

KYM: Well, geez! I know this is the dream that got this whole thing going, but it's been a couple years since you first told me and I sure didn't remember it ending like that.

DEANA: It has been a couple years, but it's still really vivid to me.

KYM: OK. So let's take a look at it. At first glance, it seems very complicated. There's a lot going on, which means that we'll take it bit by bit. Also, this seems quite different from most of the dreams that we've been working with lately. They've been mostly about processing grief and had a very differently quality.

So, let's begin with how you got back into the dream.

When you were going over your notes to remember the dream, did it bring up feelings for you? What did you feel?

DEANA: It did remind me of something that surprised me at the time. For the most part, I felt joyful because I had the talking dog. I was far less horrified by the pig man on the street than I would have expected. That bothered me a little bit, but not much. It also bothered me about what was happening to my friends and my part in it, but even then I didn't have guilt about unleashing the plague on the world. I didn't have guilt about stealing a messiah from another world. It was like I was just doing what I was doing and this was the outcome. I would have thought that that would be very disturbing to me, but it really wasn't.

KYM: When you woke up, what was the feeling?

DEANA: I felt sad that the dog couldn't talk anymore.

KYM: Okay, So there was a bit of sadness.

DEANA: Yes.

KYM: And for you, what would that dog represent?

DEANA: I very much enjoy communicating with the natural world and making organic kinds of connections, all the way from a plant to a human being. It had that kind of a feeling to me when you really connect easily and clearly, that kind of good feeling that I have in the real world when I'm able to make those connections.

Kym: Okay. If you were just to think of dogs, what does a dog mean to you?

DEANA: They're kind and loving and loyal and sweet.

KYM: All good qualities.

DEANA: Yes.

KYM: So if this dog represents you, what part of you is kind and loyal and loving and sweet?

DEANA: Well, what's really funny is that I want to define it as the part that's kind, loyal, loving and sweet.

KYM: So, when are you most naturally kind, loyal, loving and sweet?

DEANA: When I'm out interacting with the public as opposed to like when I'm in my studio creating or writing, because people will approach me all the time.

KYM: That's interesting because in this dream the people, the new people, weren't that way to you at all. In fact, they didn't even give you the time of day.

DEANA: Right.

KYM: So reaching back two years ago, can you remember someone or something, a group that was not giving you the time of day?

DEANA: My old church, they were horrible to me. And they practiced shunning.

KYM: That's interesting, because for the people in this dream, the dog was their God. Hmm...so the dog talked, right? The dog would communicate but as they unleashed the plague, it quit talking.

DEANA: Even before the plague part, I was thinking how they claim to be a group that's about love. And they claim to worship love. I believed that too, until I didn't.

KYM: And yet in this world, these people walked past the person who was totally suffering.

DEANA: They did.

KYM: Didn't help him at all.

DEANA: That's right.

KYM: Continued to worship and to love their talking dog, even though they didn't talk to each other or talk to you, but they would talk to their talking dog or their God.

DEANA: But when it comes to the point of the unleashing of the plague...

KYM: What would that be?

DEANA: I don't know.

KYM: Could that represent judgment?

DEANA: Yeah, if it is judgment that would fit. That's what I really like about this type of processing, when something comes up and you feel the fit. Anyway, it fits because I didn't feel guilty about it. I just did what I was going to do and I loved the dog. If that meant the plague came, which would totally make sense if it represents judgment, then that's the way it would be. It's kind of already unleashed and I couldn't "not" do what was in my nature to do.

KYM: That is true, but the sad part for you is the dog was going to quit talking, and was already gradually doing so.

DEANA: Yes.

KYM: So could it be that the judgment gets in the way of our communication with God, with Spirit, with something higher?

DEANA: It very much could be, especially considering that at that time I was still processing how the church I had belonged to could say one thing and behave completely different. Still coming through years of being very devoted to them, I can see how judgment does get in the way.

KYM: Okay.

DEANA: Why do you suppose the kids all turned into the giant pig person?

KYM: Why do you think that is?

DEANA: Well, if they got absorbed into that kind of belief, and I'd already decided that I wasn't going to or feel guilty about it, it would make sense. I mean I would rather you don't, but I can't do anything about that. That's your problem, not mine. Also it's a little funny to dream about talking dogs and unleashing the flea plague.

KYM: I remember at the time thinking how funny it was, but all I remembered was the talking dog.

DEANA: The other thing that was funny to me when I had the dream was that my dogs already totally talk to me. I have no trouble communicating with my pets, so it was like why would I have a dream where I think I need to go get a talking dog?

KYM: I'm glad that we're revisiting this dream because I think for instructive purposes it's good to recognize how different people process information. At the time of the dream, you were processing the feeling of disillusionment with your church, the feeling of being judged and shunned. And it came about in the metaphor of a talking dog being a god. If it were somebody else, me for example, the idea of being shunned or religious guilt or judgment would probably have been presented in an entirely different way. This is the value of talking about dreams in this way. It helps us to realize that we each have our own metaphors and thus our own dream language.

DEANA: I agree. And, it feels so interesting when you realize that you're on the right track with the dream because you can start to see the puzzle pieces come together. Even as we were talking I realized that the world in the dream was spotlessly clean, just as the church claims to be. And their houses are immaculate, but the giant writhing, suffering, pig-man on the ground, too bad for him.

KYM: I think what's also great about this particular dream, as entertaining as it is, as we talk about it, it has a very universal theme about religious guilt and judgment. Those are big issues for people, so I'm glad we went back to it.

DEANA: I am too because it really helps me see how far

I've come in letting go of the charge that I had around the church at that time. That feels really good and I think this dream was marking a turning point for me then and I hadn't really made that connection until now. How cool!

KYM: I agree. That's very cool!

Discussion Points: This dream is great fun to work with because it taps into all of Deana's imaginative skills to convey the universal message of religious guilt and judgment. First there is the lure of alternate realities when stepping through the portal and into another world, and of course, dogs that talk. Then there is the irony of the dogs being gods (dog is God spelled backward after all). And finally the apocalyptic nature of the flea plague, set about simply for loving the dog/God so much that she took it with her. Further, as the plague ensues, she feels no guilt and realizes that she was just being true to who she is. Thus this dream accomplishes a myriad of things within Deana's psyche, including seeing the religion that she had left then for what it was, and for releasing herself from the guilt and hypocrisy that had been woven into its fabric.

Chapter Six – Practice Time

Now that you've been following the process that I use when doing dream interpretation, it's your turn to give it a try. Below is another of Deana's dreams that is very brief. Let's see how you do at identifying where to jump in, what questions to ask to help lead the dreamer into awareness and finally, establishing what type of dream you think this is.

After you've worked with it yourself, go ahead and turn the page to see where it lead in the actual interpretation.

Here's the dream:

DEANA: I dreamt that I cut off my dreadlocks and I got a Mohawk and I loved it for three days. Then at the end of the third day I was horrified because, you know, dreadlocks are a big investment of time and I love them. I really wanted them back and I was just mortified that I'd cut them off. So I went to the trash and started digging around to see if I could find my dreadlocks to glue them back on. That's the whole dream.

Questions to ponder:

* What are the key components of the dream?

* Where would you begin?

* What questions would you ask?

* What words might be useful in a dream dictionary?

* What type of dream do you think this is and why?

Notes:

Actual Interpretation:

KYM: Great, okay. So there are a couple things that I land on here. The first that I would like to talk about is the dreadlocks. What do dreadlocks symbolize for you?

DEANA: To me they are the expression on the outside of who I am on the inside.

KYM: Okay, so they're expression, great. What does the Mohawk represent?

DEANA: It is playfulness, especially because I think I probably did a different color each day or did some bright, bold color. It was fun.

KYM: So Mohawk is playful and fun while the dreadlocks represent to the outside who are you on the inside. And what about three days?

DEANA: That was very significant, three days. It just kind of feels like a complete amount of time, a full cycle of time.

123

KYM: Okay. You know this because we have done quite a lot of things together, but numbers are often symbolic in and of themselves and have a meaning aside from the numerical meaning. Three is the number of communication. It's also the axis of anger and joy. With that in mind, if the Mohawk represents playfulness or joy, was there something non-joyful or angry going on in your life at the time of the dream?

DEANA: Hmmm, nothing's coming up. Not to say that things don't rattle me, but if that was what it was, I must have addressed it because it's not sticking around.

KYM: Okay. We'll go back to what you were saying, it felt like a completion. What was being completed at the time of the dream?

DEANA: Let's see. The date of the dream was very early October so I would have just recently moved out of the old studio. That felt good to have it completed, but a little nerve wracking because I didn't have the next thing lined up.

KYM: OK. So, you'd come to the end of a cycle and there were conflicting feelings. You were happy to have completed the move, but nervous because you didn't know what was coming next. How might that equate to cutting off your dreadlocks?

DEANA: Well, it could be about the time I've put into both. I'd been in the studio for 2 1/2 years. I've had the dreads for about five. Since I've been growing them, I've discovered that cutting your dreads is a reoccurring nightmare for many people with dreads because it is such an investment of time. Or, you'll dream that you're two years in and carefully comb them out or they all come out and you have to start again. It's almost like a tooth falling out for regular people, a "your dreadlocks are gone" dream for dreadlock people.

KYM: I can see how too, if this is associated with you changing your studio, it's like having to start all over again. And so here you are looking for the pieces to glue back.

DEANA: And it's from something I liked to something I liked, but there is a frustration in that, that I'm starting again, yeah, all of that work again. That has riled me up, yeah, that has. Even though I recognize I kind of have to ride that out. While I feel better about it now, at the time that I had the dream, I was more worked up about it. And now I've realized, "Yes, but if you don't have a studio finished to go to, you get to sleep in."

KYM: Good. Sounds like you've worked it out.

Discussion Points: This dream is a great example of needing to work through some unresolved nagging emotions that were frustrating Deana in her waking hours and carried over into dreamtime. These emotions are mundane, whereas in the earlier dreams, the dreams about Sadie, there was so much sorrow that was going through Deana that it spread into numerous dreams over a period of time, becoming a recurring theme. Those dreams were more complicated, deeply felt and multidimensional; while this dream is pretty straightforward in regard to just helping her process a little bit of frustration or frustrated energy that she was feeling because of the move.

Additionally, here are some good words for Deana's dictionary:

1. Dreadlocks   a) expresses on the outside who she is on the inside

                                        b) represents an investment of time and energy

2. Mohawk   a) playfulness

3. Three   a) completions of the end of a cycle.

Chapter Seven - Working With Your Dreams

Now that we've spent some time with Deana's dreams and my interpretation guidance, I hope you'll feel compelled to take a look at your own dreams. As I've mentioned several times what is most important in dream work is simply giving your attention to the significance of your dreams. In the repetition, I hope that you will remember. There is nothing magic or scientific about understanding the meaning of your dreams. It is more like getting to know a new friend who is really smart and knows a lot about you. You listen, you ask questions and you bring what they say back to yourself for awareness and growth. Your dreams, like friends, can be great company. Introduce yourself, get acquainted and get ready. The adventure starts tonight!

The tools that you will need to help get you started can be as simple as a piece of scratch paper and a pencil.

However, I recommend designating a binder, tablet or file for your dream notes. This keeps them in one place and makes future reference easier. It also helps to give form and significance to your dream memoirs.

I suggest a dream journal, such as my *"Working With Your Dreams – Companion Journal to The Lunar Key."*
In that journal there is the space for both your dream journaling and your dream dictionary. As you fill the pages, it becomes a chronicle for the narratives and the language of your subconscious mind.

To assist you, at the end of this chapter I give reminders and guidelines for both *Your Dream Journal* and *Your Dream Dictionary*. I keep these simple because this is an organic process that will evolve for you as you do it. The key is to make it fun and exciting.

Additionally, resources like Carolyn Myss' online descriptions of archetypes and Ted Andrews book, *"Animal-Speak,"* can really help to expand your interpretations. I will show you what I mean in the next dream. It is one of mine and what follows is taken directly from my dream journal. I share this as a means of illustrating dream journaling, personal interpretive application and the dream dictionary.

Here is the excerpt from my journal:

Feb. 28, 2014   *AM Dream*

I had a flash of the name Victor and in the dream state I was aware that it was short for Victory.

Sis and I were in a yard working. I was aware that whatever had gone on before, we had only done a so-so job. My back was to her but out of the corner of my eye I watched her open the shed. A blond version of Kona, Sis' chocolate lab, was by her. When she opened the shed, a bear sprang out and ran after Kona! We were shocked! In the distance we could hear chasing sounds, then fighting sounds, then chasing again. Psychically I knew that Kona and the bear were injured but that Kona had gotten away. I woke with my heart pounding and I had a vague recollection of having dreamt of a bear earlier in the week where we'd wondered if we'd locked a bear in the shed.

The dream was very deep and it took a couple hours to get my head clear.

I think that this dream represents things in my subconscious that are startling or frightening like the Bear.

*I looked up "Bear" in **"Animal Speak"** and it talked about hibernation actually being a slowing down during the winter. This made me think that it may also be a reflection of things (projects) that were started in the winter and will take shape in spring or may even take a couple years to grow to maturity (as the bear and her cubs).*

In this dream, Sis would represent the part of me that is capable, determined and gets things done.

Kona would be the part of me that is protective. She ran so the bear would chase her, then turned and confronted the bear. In the end, they were both battered but alive. This is like me when I lean into my fears, especially my subconscious fears of failure. There may be a struggle from my protective ego, but I always survive.

The feeling in the beginning of not having done our best might represent my lack of single-minded focus on my work (book?) that opened the door to my subconscious fear of failure and not being good or deserving enough. But, like the bear and its association with trees, I have to share my wisdom in order to taste the honey of success.

This dream came on the heels of an EFT session that I did around my feelings of limited financial return. So, I think that I am getting that I need to complete the cub (dream book) that I've nurtured this winter, get it out to the public, and be patient as it matures.

I must lean into my subconscious fears and trust that I will survive!

Wow! Huge Dream!

Blessed Be!

Discussion Points: First, I must admit that I wrote more about this dream than I normally might have. The intensity of the feelings it produced in combination with the out-of-character storyline, told me that I needed to spend extra time with it. Additionally, because I had had bears in two dreams, I knew that I was being directed to find out more about the bear as a messenger or totem. That is why I went to *"Animal-Speak"* for more insight. When I did that, I found myself probing more deeply what felt stalled in my life and for what might be the unconscious motivation behind the lack of inertia. That led me directly to the writing of this book and my fear of failure.

With the guidance of this dream, however, I got to see those parts of myself represented by my sister that are "capable, determined and gets things done." I also got to see my protective ego as represented by Kona. And finally, I received reassurance that this was my natural process and that I needed to continue in order to taste the sweetness of the honey, all as shown to me by the medicine of the bear.

Powerful, startling and deeply felt, this dream was most certainly a nudge from my inner healing wisdom that was telling me that it was time to lean into my fears and return to the "cub" of my creation.

From this dream came the following entries for my dream dictionary:

1. Sis   a) capable, determined, gets things done

2. Kona   a) protective, ego, survival

3. Bear   a) hibernates or slows in the winter
            b) raises her cubs to maturity (two years)
            c) climbs to the top of trees representing higher wisdom
            d) associated with the sweet reward of honey

Now, it's your turn. Your dreams are waiting. Don't feel that you have to delve as deeply as I did, at least not at first. You will get better with time and practice. As you start, just follow what feels right and you will get what you most need to know. Keep it fun. Keep it exciting. And most of all, keep at it!

Reminders

Your Dream Journal -

A Dream Journal is like a diary where you write down the important aspects of a dream, including dates, details, feelings and thoughts from, or about, the dream.

These can be valuable in later reflection when looking for patterns and providing context for how they may be tied to your waking experiences. I recommend that you keep your entries brief. However, you will find what works for you.

I generally write about the dream first and then I go back and start working with the interpretation, if it hasn't already hit me. Sometimes just giving it form by putting it into words and on paper, the meaning and purpose just pop out. Other times it takes more work.

Your Dream Dictionary -

Once you begin to keep track of your dreams, you will start to see the emergence of certain symbols that will repeat themselves and that will have a unique meaning to you. For example, a cat meant one thing to Deana, but it might have a different meaning for you. Keeping track of that meaning can help you make quicker interpretations when those symbols appear in other dreams.

In addition to personal symbols, you might also see archetypal or universal symbols appear. If some of the people, places or things in your dreams don't seem to have a personal application, I would suggest that you get a book or do an online search on the possible archetypal meaning behind the symbol and then ask, "How is this representative of me?" Then, as with personal symbols, keep track of the meaning in your dream dictionary for future reference.

Chapter Eight - Reaching Within the Depths

I was in a meditation induced nap, not yet dreaming, but thinking of Will. My heart leaned toward heaviness, as I was beginning to drift into the detachment of sleep.

Suddenly I hear, "Hi Auntie Kymmie!" and I look into the vastness of darkened space and I see him! Will is floating and twisting and twirling in the air! His smile is broad and his heart feels light. Immediately I'm light too, but fearful at the same time that I will somehow ruin this moment. I say, "Please help me." He reaches out his hand and takes mine. Without a word, we move up and up until we come to a rickety flight of stairs. They remind me of Dr. Seuss stairs and I smile. We begin to walk up the stairs, hand in hand, Will in the lead. It's feeling lighter and lighter and finally we reach the top. We step onto the threshold and in that moment Will is gone. I think I'm going to be sad, but then I realize that I feel peaceful. It becomes dark and I am at peace.

I wake up…again with tears in my eyes, but his time they are tears of gratitude and joy for getting to see Will again. Like the first dream, there is little talk, but this time it didn't seem to matter. The feeling of joy and lightness was everywhere and I wanted to breathe it in and become it. His voice saying, "Hi Auntie Kymmie!" was so sweet; it still rings in my ears and sounds in my heart…a precious gift.

This dream brought me great resolution and has helped me through the months after Will's death to remember his joyfulness, then and now. It gave me the reassurance that Will is happy and free and that he is just beyond the veil of physical reality. He is there and I can hear him say, "Hi Auntie Kymmie!"

That is the truth that I know beyond all certainty. It is most personal and yet transpersonal. It came to me in a dream and I took the time to listen.

Epilogue

Today is August 4, 2014. It is raining and has been all day. This is both unusual and welcome in the state of Nevada where rain is rare, especially rain that stays all day.

I got up early and felt the delicious and moist cool of the morning. I breathed it in and let my shoulders drop. For a couple weeks prior to today, there had been both an internal and external tension building that had kept me on edge. Unlike today, the weather had been hot, humid and charged with an electric energy. Mirroring my internal state, I felt like it might suffocate me if it didn't break free. I longed for the rain and the release of the building pressure, both inner and outer.

I hadn't realized how on edge I'd been, until I wasn't, and I issued a prayer of gratitude for the rain. Just as everything is connected, I know that the rain and I are one.

As it releases, I release. Just like Jake's *Lunar Tear*, it is both happy and sad. I know this and I am grateful for both.

Yesterday would have been Will's 25th birthday, the first since his passing. Each of the "firsts" is unbearable in thought, until it happens and then we move through it and go on. I realize now that I had been holding my breath for weeks hoping that I could make this day bearable for my sister. And of course, I couldn't do that, only she could. Only my sister could do the work to prepare herself for this day, and she did…somehow we all did.

A small, close group of family and friends got together and did a wonderful ritual that Will would have loved. We called it "Art & Fire" and it was profound. And I read my dream to the group for the first time, choking over Will's words, "Hi, Auntie Kymmie." It was a vulnerable moment for me as I shared the very personal yet transpersonal nature of the experience. But how could I not? Will gave me that gift and I had to share it.

Each day I continue to learn so much about myself from Will's life and from his death. And now, I am learning from him in my dreams.

About the Author

Spiritual teacher, integrative life coach and author, **Kym Maehl** was born in the United States and has worked with groups and individuals worldwide in assisting authentic transformation. In addition to her private practice as a counselor and life coach, she teaches classes in integrative wellness modalities and the creative arts. She holds a PhD in Holistic Ministries, an MA in Counseling and Educational Psychology, and is a Certified Clinical Hypnotherapist, Rehabilitation Counselor, and Strategic Life Coach.

Kym is passionate about the need for inspired holism in both individual and collective consciousness and it is her goal to advance awareness by teaching, coaching, and providing accessible and thought-provoking courses and seminars. She currently resides with her husband and transformational astrologer, Ron Maehl, just over the hill from her beloved Lake Tahoe in Carson City, Nevada.

For more information go to:

http://spiritcounseling.org/about_us

www.ingramcontent.com/pod-product-compliance
Lightning Source LLC
LaVergne TN
LVHW041223080426
835508LV00011B/1062